D1385138

DOVER PICTORIAL ARCHIVE SERIES

GEOMETRIC DESIGN AND ORNAMENT

374 COPYRIGHT-FREE DESIGNS FOR ARTISTS AND CRAFTSMEN

Selected by
EDMUND V. GILLON JR.

Dover Publications, Inc.
New York

Published in Canada by General Publishing Company, Ltd., 30 Lesmill Road, Don Mills, Toronto, Ontario.
Published in the United Kingdom by Constable and Company, Ltd., 10 Orange Street, London WC 2.

Geometric Design and Ornament is a new work, first published by Dover Publications, Inc., in 1969. The illustrations in this volume have been selected from *Ornament* by Y. Chernikhov, published (in Russian) by the author in Leningrad in 1930.

DOVER *Pictorial Archive* SERIES

Standard Book Number: 486-22526-7
Library of Congress Catalog Card Number: 76-97126

Manufactured in the United States of America
Dover Publications, Inc.
180 Varick Street
New York, N.Y. 10014

8

14

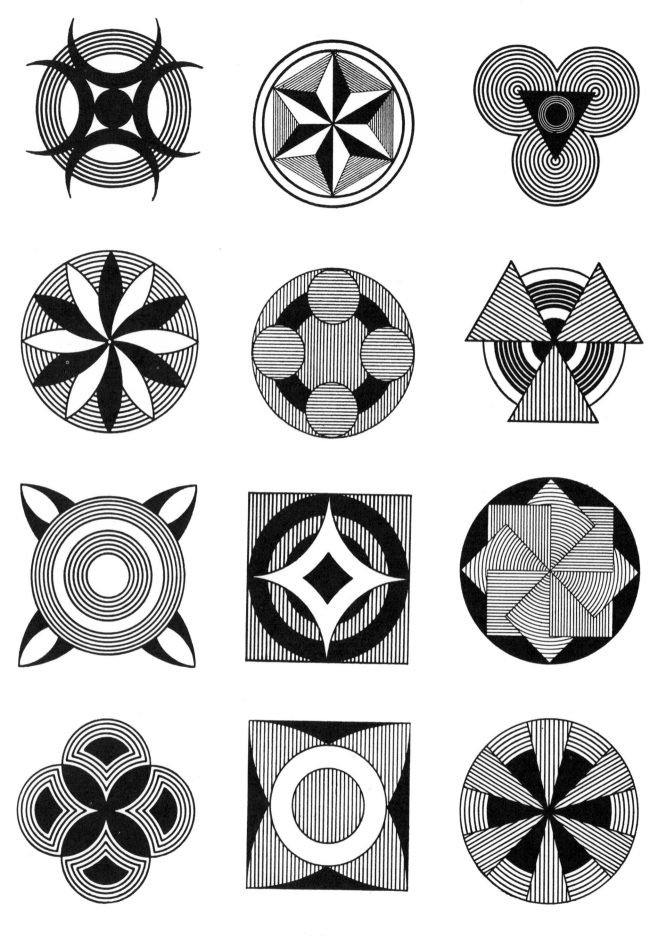

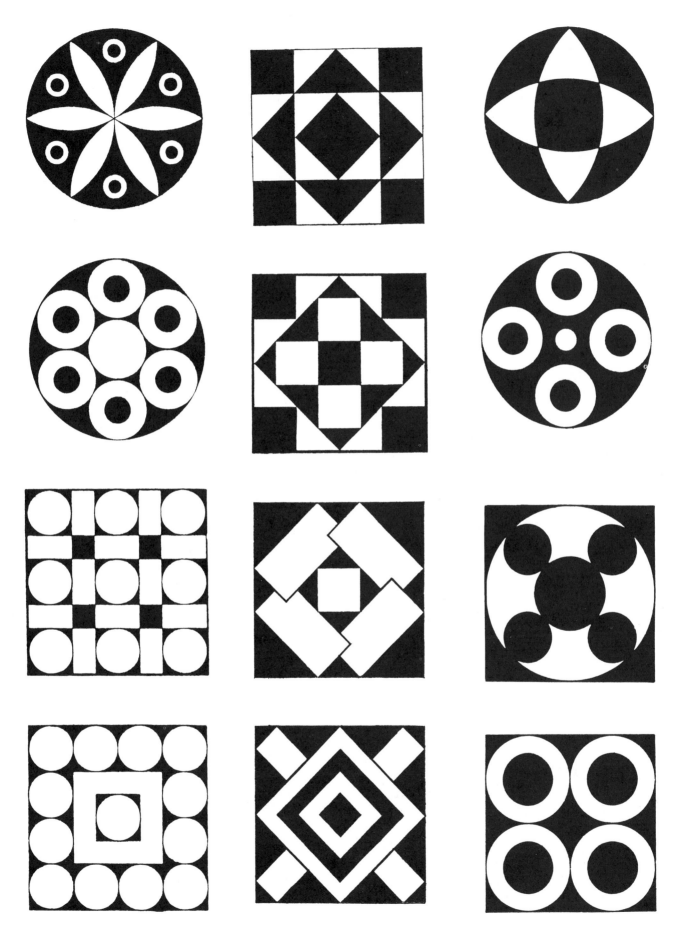

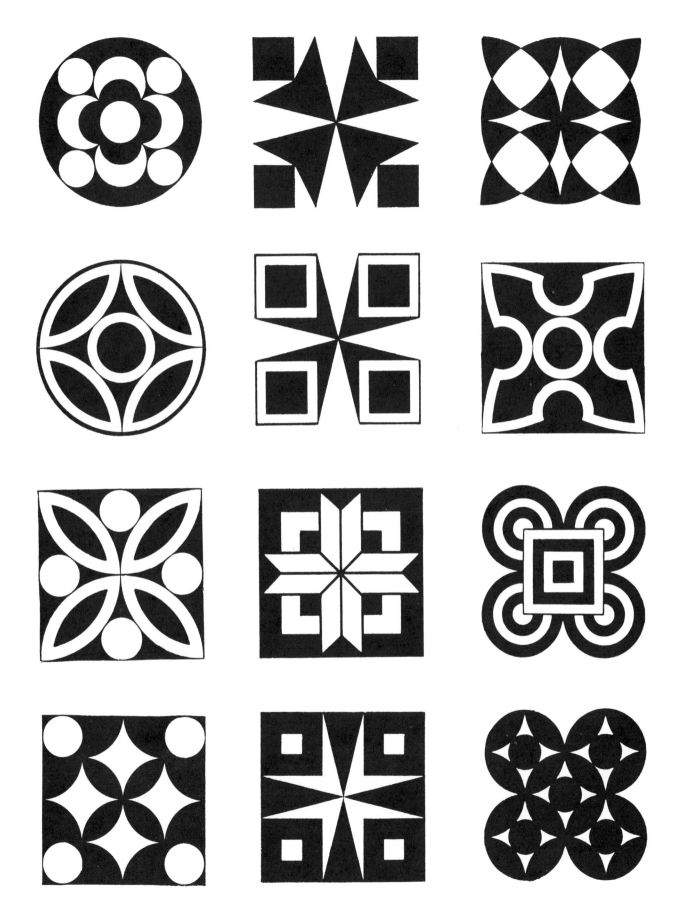

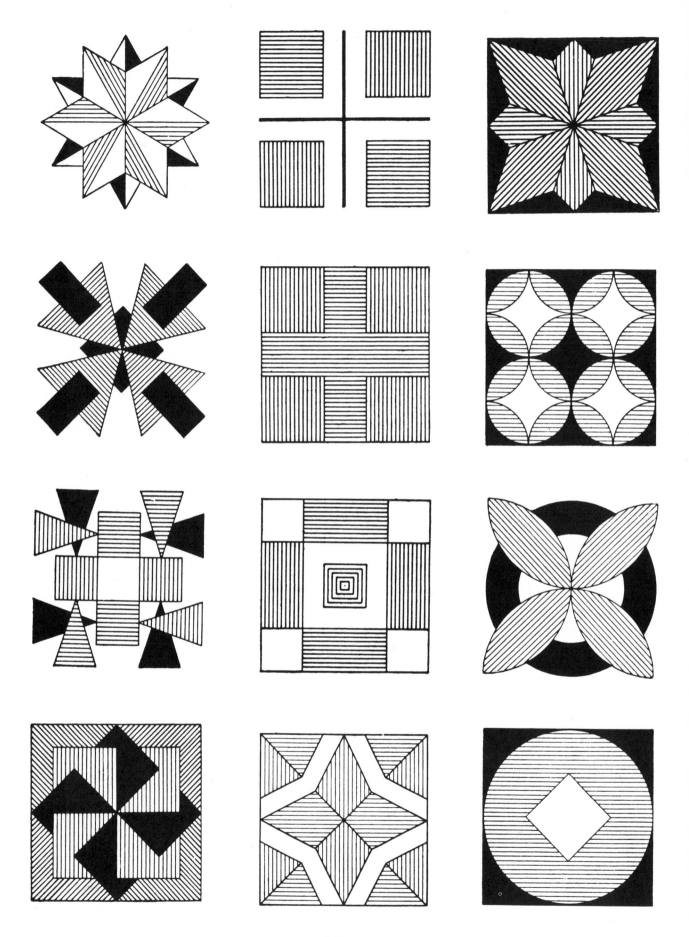

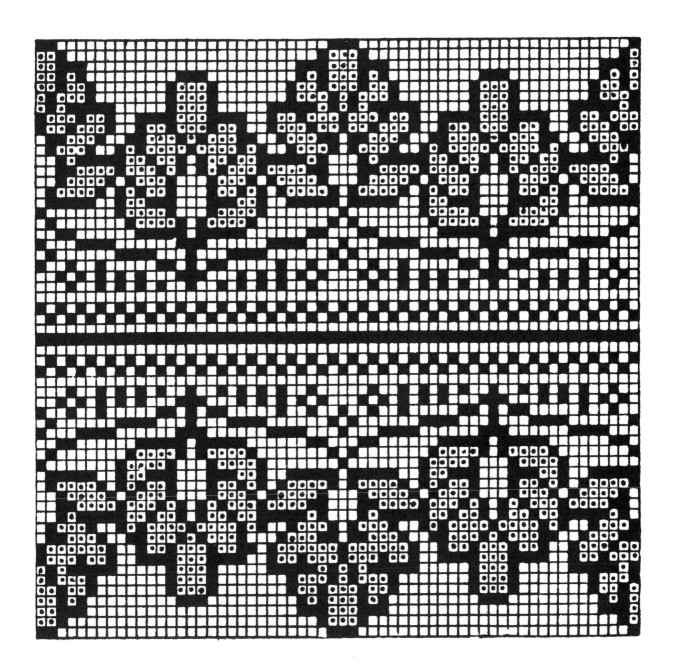

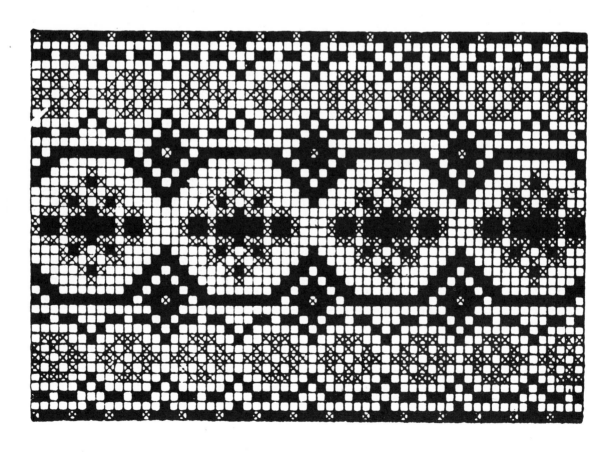

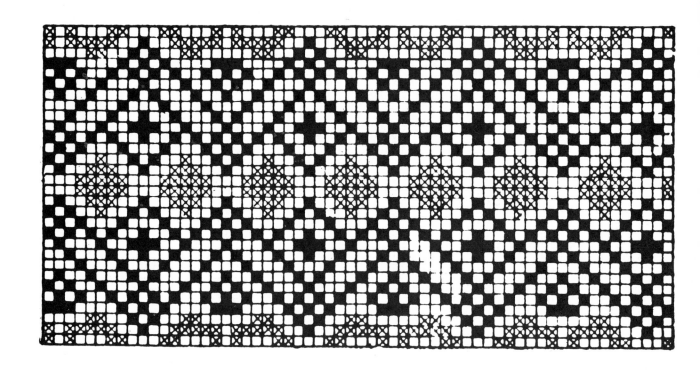

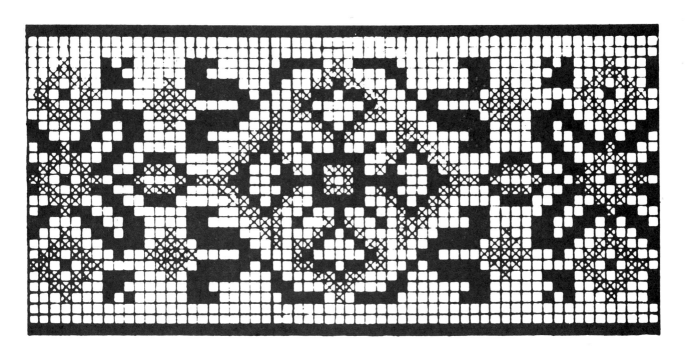

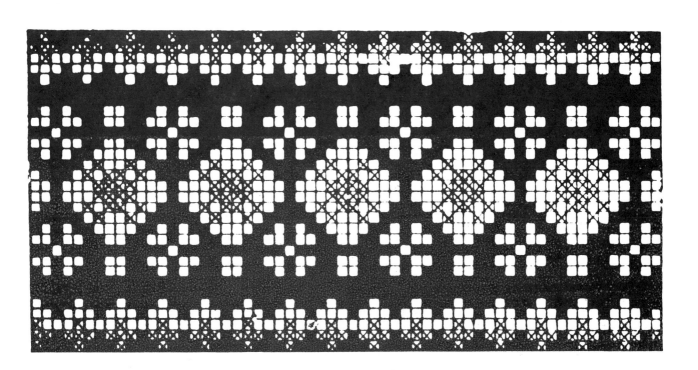

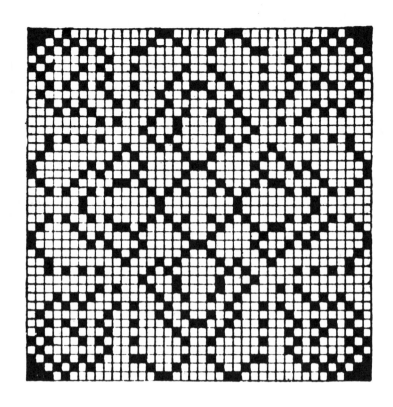

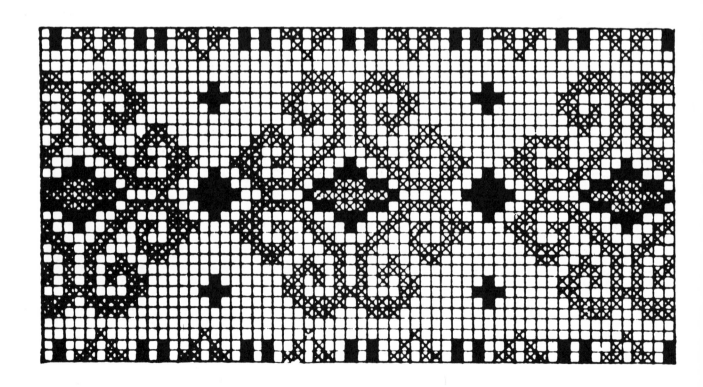

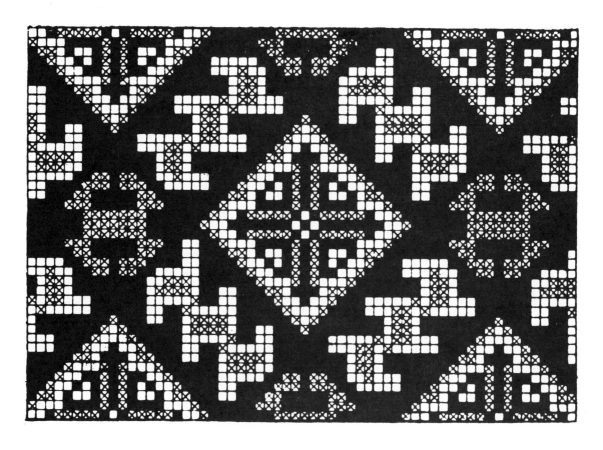

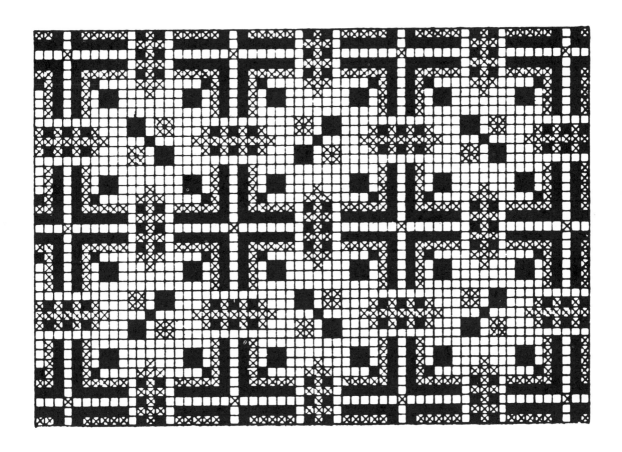

54

63

65